my itty-bitty bio

LeBron James

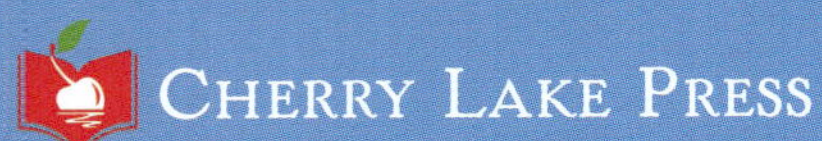

Published in the United States of America by Cherry Lake Publishing
Ann Arbor, Michigan
www.cherrylakepublishing.com

Reading Adviser: Beth Walker Gambro, MS, Ed., Reading Consultant, Yorkville, IL
Illustrator: Leo Trinidad

Photo Credits: © Sean Pavone/Shutterstock, 5; © ZUMA Press, Inc./Alamy Stock Photo, 7; © Cinematic/Alamy Stock Photo, 9; © ZUMA Press, Inc./Alamy Stock Photo, 11, 22; © AP Photo/Matthew Hinton/ASSOCIATED PRESS, 13; © A.RICARDO/Shutterstock, 15; © AP Photo/Mark J. Terrill, ASSOCIATED PRESS,17, 23; © AP Photo/Mark Duncan/ASSOCIATED PRESS, 19; © UPI/Alamy Stock Photo, 21

Cherry Lake Press is an imprint of Cherry Lake Publishing Group

Library of Congress Cataloging-in-Publication Data has been filed and is available at catalog.loc.gov.

Printed in the United States of America

table of contents

About the author: When not writing, Dr. Virginia Loh-Hagan serves as the Executive Director for AANAPISI Affairs and the APIDA Center at San Diego State University. She is also the Co-Executive Director of The Asian American Education Project. She lives in San Diego with her very tall husband and very naughty dogs.

About the illustrator: Leo Trinidad is a *New York Times* bestselling comic book artist, illustrator, and animator from Costa Rica. For more than 12 years, he's been creating content for children's books and TV shows. Leo created the first animated series ever produced in Central America and founded Rocket Cartoons, one of the most successful animation studios in Latin America. He is also the 2018 winner of the Central American Graphic Novel contest.

my story

I was born in 1984. I was born in Akron.

Akron is in Ohio.

I grew up poor. I’m close with my mother.

She gives me strength.

DESTINATION
FINALS
DESTINATION
FINALS

I started playing basketball at age 9. I played in high school.

I was a star.

Do you play sports?

I play **professional** basketball. I broke many records. I won many games.

I am a champion.

LAKERS
23

I am the top scorer. I can score from anywhere on the court.

I am one of the greatest players.

LAKERS
23

I played in the **Olympics**. I did this four times.

I won medals.

USA
6

I love my family. I married my high school girlfriend.

My sons play basketball, too.

I have **social media** fans. I am a community leader. I support my **hometown**.

I have opened schools.

What is your hometown?

My legacy lives on.

I am a role model.

What would you like to ask me?

timeline

2020

1980

Born
1984

2023

2080

glossary & index

glossary

hometown (HOHM-TOWN) the place where someone was born

Olympics (uh-LIM-piks) international sports contests held every 4 years

professional (pruh-FESH-nuhl) related to a job; describing when someone is paid for their work

social media (SOH-shuhl MEE-dee-uh) websites and apps where people can create and share content

index